AF521662

STRAY

ADAM HOULE

LITHIC PRESS
FRUITA, COLORADO

STRAY

Design & layout by Kyle Harvey

STRAY
Adam Houle
ISBN 978-0-9975017-1-1
Lithic Press

For my friend, writing partner, and wife, Landon

CONTENTS

North Is Looking Up

Stray

Husbandry

STRAY

NORTH IS LOOKING UP

SOLITUDE'S BEST APPRENTICE

Always the basement work of winter nights,
my father's hands to the bench stone
honing his good knives' burred edges

picked from wraps of worn denim. Blades
he tended for the one sure cut where
and when he'd need it. Chisels, gouges, sloyds

for stop cuts, their fishtail handles oversized
to better turn their leverage in tight spaces.
He shaved back each peel thin as parchment.

Cut after slim cut, his hands trained the shape,
freeing what it was he saw or thought he saw:
a mongrel dog. A mask. Wood, he knew,

is flexible as a man needs. It breathes
through its grain, fiddlebacks swirled like tight
curls on a child. Once, he crafted a man,

a clown hobo I now see he fashioned
from my face, a willow pole shouldered,
nameless fish hanging from the clenched

heart of his hand. My father, solitude's
best apprentice, mastering the world's
first craft, apprenticed me in turn.

In that flood-lit basement, his knives
lined the table, patient as black ice
on the marsh road. With the night's last cut,

he passed where I sat on the stairs. I went down,
thumbed his work. Now I shush the broom
and gather tailings, just as I was taught.

STARING DOWN

My rosary-wrapped hands in my lap. Forgive me,
        Father, these are wreckful hands, and busy.

DISCIPLINE HEARING

Res Life fumes.
It wants to rasp your teeth

to blunt nubs.
Consider the whiteness of the wall—

what pureness, that polar expanse
as the hearing screws down to brass tacks.

Past the one window, a dogwood's naiveté
is your native, grateful disposition.

Oh, hayseed, hayseed, my hayseed,
be half-hatched, be half-compliant,

wrap half your crown in quilts.
Say it: I quit. I quit. I quit. It's a hard

frost, kid, that balls its fist.
A squall line spells your name

then the winds efface it.
Past the fence line, past campus, you watch

a black dog unthread its head from its collar
after—but what effort!—it failed to snap its chain.

A PAPER HIVE EARNS NO QUARTER

It's hell, I think, to see them flit that way
at dusk back to us, swarming our willow
where, limb-perched, they flex in shadows. You pray
they quit us; I pump the poisoned bellows.
Love, things can grow too large for us to love,
so let my labor *mean.* I'm wreathed in smoke,
an axe-handle clenched in a leather glove.
You cough and gripe. I give the nest a poke
then, cocking back, let loose a full-on swing.
It all explodes. They're too smoke-drunk to know
it's me they hate and fail to sink a sting.
The job is done. I clasp the bellows closed.
Look, wife: dazed on your chipped garden gnome
one dumb wasp thinks she drives her stinger home.

WE'D LEARN LATER HER HUSBAND LEFT

Though we were young and knew little,
we were good Catholics, and kind, taught
to work in quiet, and when we did talk
to talk from below so that each exchange
took place on a gentle slope, an inclined plane
or pulley system, a simple machine,
like one of history's many that's kept
the species ticking. So we were ticking
when Teacher Nancy turned her attention
to somewhere above our heads, a point beyond
us. She cried quietly as the room shushed
with the soft whisper of safety scissors
that snipped to shape Noah's felt animals.
I—more than most—loved her and wondered
as I cut who I could hurt to stop her hurt,
sure that some violence God could endorse,
that mercy's counterweight is just and swift.
That I, in my kindness, must deliver it.

THE ONE WHERE THE GIRL DIED IN WOODS CLOSE TO HOME

It started when a filament popped
in the lone headlight
of the snow sled,

quietly, beneath the engine's roar
and the grind of the single-track
trundle churning snow

as the girl left late
to make it home.
The blizzard, my mother

says, buried her
back-trail and without
a light she could not find

her trace. That filament,
the fine hair finely split,
brought on a deeper night,

and with it the wind conspired.
The wind banked great drifts.
It rearranged the known world's face.

BEE: LATE SEASON

After the first frost I'm an air slug.
Bloated with cold, I ache in my sugar
frock of bones. Too many bristles
stiffen even as I work to bristle,
a signal for someone to warm me.

A fine but finite design, good to work
or guard the summer's work,
our flitting straight-laced factory—
there is always much to do
while warm days let us do it.

Caught in the first frost I slug
it out for dawn, drone along,
numb, nearly mindless, and hum
to warm until I feel another hum,
a stuttering day, the watery sun.

Who's not saved far from home
will never know what *lost* means;
a lone finite dance, the one map
I draw, is worth less than I had hoped.
Toward a stranger home I home.

GUNFLINT RANGE

So damn damp, the spitting sleet
that pelts then glazes all the roads.
Take this frozen pond of a parking lot,
the gas pumps an aviary of grounded
birds with long necks, beaks ice-slick,
sleek as the glossy magazine bodies
racked inside the empty, well-lit station.
He mops the day's boot grime, treads
kicked of slush and road salt, floors
buffed until they flush a dancehall shine.
Admires his work and grows bored,
thumbs the well-thumbed pages
looking for someone to look back. Looking
for some tune in the endless fluorescent hum.
Third shift, a study in discord that turns
more lonesome in each blast of wind
hauling its cold freight across the foothills.
Temperatures drop and keep dropping.
The one trucker long since bedded up.
His sleeper's cab a nest of sleeping bags,
Guns 'n' Roses, porno. Someone
should slash the truck's tires
before morning, or he'll be left nothing
but the snow-chains' hard bite in fresh snow.

ELEGY WITH CIGARETTES AND FOLDING CHAIRS

Dwayne, assistant supervisor for second shift
at Woodland Manor, took two chairs
from Ted's room after he died, the family
wanting only photos of themselves
and valuables. The chairs they left
with the bed, the books, his sailor's chest,
so Dwayne carried the chairs to the porch
where my grandmother, Ted's nursing
home girlfriend, and widow Jackie took
in the Wisconsin spring, smoking
their three allotted cigarettes. Sometimes,
I'd visit, bring extra smokes, a six pack,
and sprawl on the cooling concrete,
pleased to be someone's guest as shadows
stretched the reach from St. Paul's,
across the lot and the cars, and kept
toward us all, a blight of chill the blind
women blamed on cloud weather
and not the sure advance of night.
Other times, I could be no one's friend
and sat in my truck and drank, watching them
tilt their faces toward the sun's remainder.
How sure they tugged at their shawls.
Then, it was good Dwayne's arm to usher
his wards through the late well-lit halls.

HOW MY GRANDFATHER THOUGHT ABOUT INTELLIGENT DESIGN

It started with knowing male from female. Discerning

pipes with penises from pipes with vaginas
and which snug best with which, a love story.

Years he handcarted the Soo Line
tracking the flight of grouse roused—one hand

an extended cap brim—in a whir of gear
and leverage. Tiny pistons of birds he forged

into parables, never once reconciling
the glinting straight line of track

pontooned through pine swamps
with how it might feel to soar like scattershot

into the fractures of fugitive rays.

THE HORSESHOE

The light fades late in north Wisconsin.
Long summer days linger over pine,
and the birch swamps wash in weak sun
like the sun you'd see in a movie
where a man or prodigal dog picks
a path through the hummocks
toward home after being gone
a long time. By the time the light
is gone, no one's come. You drink,
throw horseshoes, and only know
ringers by their *clings* and sparks
when the prong catches the pin.
Each muscle remembers what it did
and can do it again. They remember
clutch and release, the arm outstretched
after the shoe leaves, like it wants back
what's sailing past your grip.

CONSIDERATIONS FOR MAKING ODDS ON THE IDITAROD

Helicopters drop bedding and fresh booties
for the dogs along the route for days.
Checkpoints of the Interior, where vets
fret the hearts and feet of the huskies
for bad valves or fractures, a shoulder
bit too deeply by the harness.
Moose will scatter a team, crush the lead
into the snow, stomp a skull or shatter
the backbones of a dog too slow
in his sidestep, the dance of flesh and hoof
strung out along the line. The bite
of the sled blades, too, finding purchase
on sharp curves that lurk in a blizzard,
undetected. To set off into all that white
is an act of faith. Hope is a yawning fissure
waiting mid-river to swallow dawn whole.
A last green dance, the Northern Lights' twirl.

BLACK ICE AND THE JAWS OF LIFE

After another Genevieve failure
I am heading wherever for a change.
Goodbye is a travel mug bounced off
the crown of my head. A finale fine
and swift, the sort of gesture a man
can remember. Like the first time

I spun out on the marsh road,
flailed and broke my nose
hoping to shield the wheel's blow.

Ice-fogged dawn, you should forewarn
when it all will jack-knife
into a bar ditch during a hard snow.

And tell me how much later until a stranger
finds me buckled and bloody, hanging
there, the radio squawking sports talk
while the yellow beams of headlights
pierce a bog of failed cranberries,
those ice-crusted swamps, fallow, fallow.

NORTH IS LOOKING UP

At Wetmore the cliffs are undercut
by Superior's ice. Shoving its elbows
shoreward, the lake scoops great bowls
in the mudstone until the roots of spruce
freeze, dark as frost-bit fingers.

Here I grew to know
a snow-buried pinecone's crunch
beneath my sturdy boots.
At early dusk, walking the shoreline
as scalloped clouds thickened to the north

I think of all the tankers sunk
in those waters so cold the bodies of sailors
fail to decompose. Down there they soak,
floating in boiler rooms, sleeping quarters.
Taconite heavy in the hulls and undelivered.

South of the Soo Locks, where the wind socks
flap orange on all that water, the Erie
and Ohio ore docks still wade in their rust.
All night ice groans, and the cold
could shatter a man if the wind turns

North to shear the coast, finds him
studying the split twists of windfalls
as night falls. A crow's nest snatched
from its heights. Sleet slanting
through the pine grove needles the skin.
Needles fall encased in ice.

THE FUTURE TIMBER BARON WRITES HIS NEW WIFE

As sure as my fidelity I wake
at the timberline so cold it strikes me
how warm you must feel elsewhere.
It's squalor: the camp, my men,
the wide-eyed girl they found
in Yellowknife, the one they kidnapped
or who tagged along, who brews
a gritty cup and gathered
her skirts to squat at the stove
until a slighter man loaned
a pair of trousers, a rope run
through the belt loops. Her coffee,
a far cry from the cups we'd take
at the Harrington with its lush,
deep carpet I imagine you gliding
across as the heads of men turn
from their women and their friends,
burns my tongue and doesn't last.
It's a sad lot to find me gone
to secure the future of our home.
Truly, a white city on a hill in spring,
you are a boulevard that is leaf-lined,
trim, and clean. It's all I can do to keep
the saw teeth biting and free of rust.
Such tough timber to haul and pulp
for the scented paper that sells so well
back East. Christ, these new mules
mucking logs into the valley. You'd think
they were asses the way they bray
when they bog in a sink. Yesterday,
just yesterday, the Yellowknife girl
helped me anchor the supply tent
in a squall. When she stretched to lash
the hemp around a bough, her sleeves
rose at wrists so pale and thin and taut
I could not help but sigh. Then work harder.

IN LIEU OF FLOWERS,

the general's winter lemons
packed in a munitions crate
tamped shut with square nails

for the conscripted men
to suck in wedges, boots
propped on a rail of snake fence.

When they finish, let them lob
the spent meat and mumped skin
like grapeshot. Let them laugh

a boy's laugh as they try to bull's-eye
their cuts of sun on the peaceable backs
of those grazing, broad-faced ponies.

STRAY

The town where our parents moved us
fringed a tall and darksome city.

Not the town they promised.
My sisters and I grew furious,

thistle in the constant northern shade.
We stole and shattered glass

at every chance, slammed our father's
three-pound sledge on Mason jars

we cradled off pantry shelves.
When our mother's back was turned

from her work at the stainless double sinks
and the high-set kitchen window framed

our legs shredding air past the swings
we practiced the middle finger,

that singular piston.
Rage our new order. Our eyes shone

like polished steel, flecks of mettle
spreading. We learned to bristle

like wild dogs, cleaved spirits
of coal, of indomitable industry.

STRAY

BEGGING HOME A STRAY

I'm told in Ralls this county coughs
its dogs up roadside, whole litters
left in a burst of exhaust, road
dust, as if death is less pressing
through the terms of practice.
At the county line, though, it's just one
brindle pit, a four-finger gap
between his eyes, shrunk withers
like fresh razors in the high
headlights of trucks. A red
sun crests the low clouds.
So I call to him, try treats, ride.
Say, *you're a good boy, let's go*
home now. My heart's odometer
rolls to zeros, and still
he'll have none of it, shies
on thin hips as I ease closer.
Oh, shovel-head, oh bull terrier
of our interminable nights, try
to believe there's home yet to come
home to, a vast and verdant yard.
Think of the tennis balls, the rope
toys, the greed that drives you
to love the tug-of-war. And prairies,
dog, where you run for running's sake,
grasses trembling with all you have
left unnamed. I'll call a new name
as you scent the far-ranging winds
for rumor of all that has been
lost. Look around, damn you. I'm it.
We're out here. I am what you found.

TO THE BED BUG

Little buddy chugging
innocuously enough
beneath my cotton sock,

tag-a-long armed
with anticoagulant
and an endless gut,

welcome to me,
a humble type-O host.
My blood is your blood,

eh, *ami?* Or is it *amie?*
Classy, aren't I?
Urbane and friendly,

worrying French gender
that way. You're worth it,
best lesson in commensalism.

I get you. I've taken
the orphan's clingy ride
with style, rendered myself

immune to all but need.
I, like you, work to keep
a bleeder gently bleeding.

YELLOWKNIFE GIRL AT THE TIMBER CAMP

Cook looked to me to find some wild onion.
Scoffed and spit when I told there were none
and quit to his pallet off the wood room, drunk.
I worried but he didn't stray to my bunk
where I waited for dawn to show my breath,
white, rising. As he slept, I dressed, left
to scour the woods, camp's best rifle slung
at my back to drop a buck on his run
but I saw none. Only ice-rimed creeks
shallow at the edges and, at the center, so deep
a fist-sized rock looked like a pebble. The first
pale crocus near a twisted pine had burst
through snow, soft as new cloth. I plucked it.
Loathe what wilts before the melt. I crushed it.

EARTHWORM FLOODED OUT IN RAIN

I think you should make a fine snake
someday, a tree-dweller whose gulleted
jaw draws down the jay's eggs whole.
Think it: basking in high branches,
alight in the dappled light that's dappled
just like the pattern your skin will take
in place of the purplish, crinkled mess
of *is* and *is.* I'm certain your new skin
will become you and become you again
for years, those broad belly scales well fit
to compel you along a chosen path,
branch to branch and down to birdbath,
under fences or over, or through the slats
if you care to flatten your ribs and squeeze.
Hell, coil and strike from a bottle
if you want to. This death's worth it, worm—
you won't aerate the garden. You'll own it.

ON TOUCHING MY DOG'S COLD AND PERFECT TEETH

I hum Ruby Tuesday when I think of dying.
No more tired homecomings to this herder
in the hall, her nails tapping their code
of love and need across the hardwood.
No whining, no mad scrabble as she gains
her feet and storms the steps, glad I'm alive
and home, no matter what I've done.
I fret housefires too. Flames climbing
the walls, flames fanned by wind
through a leaky window. Would she blame
me for a bad outlet and crosswords
stacked on a bedside table? Most nights
I keep watch and heft my share of grace,
listen for the click of the pilot light.
Through open vents the forced air rises.

DECEMBER, ICE STORM

The limber yearling bows beneath the weight
of inch on inch of ice, a supplicant
who, arriving, would now prefer escape.
Revise the rapture. Cue up puzzlement
with sleet's tinny song on the shed's pocked tin
and groans of stubborn limbs that refused to give.
My neighbor thought to heat up gasoline
on the kitchen stove–which but served to prove
that *want-to* doesn't mean the same as *must*–
to warm his truck's hard engine so he'd make it
to Shakers, where he stared but swore *they sluts.*
Better to ignore your twig than slake it.
I glide the yard to watch his trailer burn:
stairs lead to flames and air, rails black as scorn.

CONFESSIO INIMICUS

Fairy-winged brightly green thing,
I'm sorry it's come to a thumb
rolled over you, crushing
your armor-clad organs
beneath my one-offed ridges,
and as I snuff you out I think
of the tired cop who blotted
in order each of my fingers,
then my palm's hard heel,
and, last, the knife blade
of my hand, pinky tip to wrist,
as I small-talked her to ease
the shame of my booking
just like I small-talk you now
when I grind the last of your shell
to the tawny, textured wall
of this modest home I own,
papers hold my name's scrawl
like the bit of guts you leave:
that matters to me, not much,
but some, and there's a database
now that knows me by the contour
lines of my fist when it's forced
open to scan my hand's topography—
here an oxbow, here a swirl,
here a glacial scar carved across a whorl—
and now, now you know me too,
you careless insect, I bet
you wish you never trespassed,
flat now as a dead-eyed mug shot,
but I'm sorry it's come to this
bad end to a life's messy sentence,
splice after splice after splice
until a wrong-timed period.
I meant what I did.
I mean what I say.

AFTER WATCHING A K-9 ASSAULT DEMONSTRATION AT LACKLAND AFB, 1967

Back north, we'd praise soft teeth
in a dog, and a sleek body
paddling a steaming marsh at dawn,
a Goldeneye nested between
the gentle jaws that could but didn't
splinter bone into the meat.

Our best dog kept the bird unbruised,
that's what my father taught.
He held up in the blind's smoky light
each drake or hen Sissy brought in
and twisted the wing to gauge how hard
she clutched the bird. She got good

quick, sparse praise alone urging
her release. He'd say, *That's how it's done.*
I believed him. Believed I always would.

PHOTO OF MY FATHER AT FIFTY SEEING THE GRAND CANYON FOR THE FIRST TIME

As he braces a rail on South Rim
near the mouth of Bright Angel
Trail you're left believing
he dug the damn hole himself,
finishing the job just before
the shutter snapped shut
on a duck-stance and a grin
that suggest, if not by his design,
then by one he saw and signed for
allowed for the labor we mistake
to call a natural marvel. I imagine
my father and the river, both young,
both tired but glad they were hired,
sipping MGD after the first day's work
was done. There's a gully behind
them, a wet scratch in raw earth,
really, and my father proudly shows
the river his clay-caked, blistered
hands. His sleeves are rolled
to the elbow, his ropey forearms
taut as guy-wires. His plans
are huge, he tells the river as much,
then they're cutting up like boys
when a blister pops and cannot
stop its weeping through his fist.

THE REDDISH CUR

Out she clambers
from beneath the keel-up canoe
left to rot in switch grass

and is not the lone fox the cops
first thought. Agents, noose snares
and tranquilizers, voices

that fracture the radio wire
converge. All these trappings
of capture after a woman

is yoked down on a dead-end
Georgia road by a pack of dogs
gone mad for lack of collars,

lack of names. After the first lunge
there's no quit. They mauled the man
who hoped to bring her home.

The disastrous plays good odds.
Then happens. Then happens again.
The rest is aftermath, and that jaw-snap

dance of teeth and fur rises
to meet the county's men
sent to collect and kill.

They rise as one except that one
reddish cur, who looks back, then leaves
through spindled trees behind the canoe,

slinks and disappears into shadow
hemmed by splintered fence posts.

STARING DOWN

Hard veins roped forearm to wrist—
    snare lines hitching when I make a fist.

BIRD. PILGRIM. WATER.

–On the Goodnight-Loving Trail

If mud leaks from the mouth of a dauber,
it comes to you from the closest water.

Line up its flight straight back above the prayer
of winds that scythe the prairie grass and start,
circumspect, afraid of snakes. Who cares where
the damn bird's headed—worry, parched heart,

where it's been, what playa or bitter wallow
it knows that you don't. Become the cast shadow

of the swallow cutting free its back trail.
To save what's left at a shallow lake
you must wade, bootless, your shirt a wet veil
of sweat shrouding your face. If it should take

all day to reach the water, it's time well spent.
Ablution's not for you unless it's lent.

THE SLOW PROMENADE OF ARMADILLOS

Cloaked officiants pushing north.
A bumbling of accidentals wed
to success. Or a suspect success,
its genesis rooted in accident.
Even the doubtful must know
them by their bands of scutes,
their oblong wobble on a gravel
shoulder at dusk. Rejoice in her,
a lone armadillo rustling thistle,
unconcerned that you are there.
How ordained it starts to feel,
those mission-driven mendicants
who forage and grunt at garbage dumps.
Pity them their flooded land bridge.
No route home shows itself,
so they grow lean in their hard skin
and learn to wade the waters
of a shallow stream to reach what's good
in the fields beyond. The desolate offices
they keep are tended as well as any
warren. Witness as one stretches
to climb a fence: an accordion
in the Lord's wind, a hardback hymnal
opening, taut and self-explained.

HUSBANDRY

WE IN THE REPUBLIC

The pecan grove is merely warm.
Boughs, stretched and heavy
with the hard fruit, stitch

shade across the tended plot.
Beyond, a scorched range
dotted with cacti patches

blackened by disease—
pads dropped by drought—
rolls toward the road.

In the county's crushed gravel,
the blood of a prairie dog
dries and leaves no stain.

Like four pins in a ruined cushion,
limbs reach, the dead fending
off a truck that got to work

on time. A scarecrow animate,
another dumb drifter, dust streaked,
gains over the blasted landscape,

lingers at the fence line.
He pops nails with a cat's paw
and fills two filthy milk jugs

at a drip hose. A slow process
he passes by cracking pecans,
plucking string from hems, an offering

to the few song birds nesting above.
They will take up the dingy ribbons.
Those scant flags mark what they own.

WORK / WORK BALANCE

By the time you're home,
the floors have sunk an inch to sub-rot.
Big deal, right? They've slipped a bit.

And what doesn't give beneath your weight?
The windows will not glide their frames.
The neighbor dogs are hoarse.

They sound asthmatic, like it burns
to bark but would hurt worse
if they resigned themselves to silence.

So welcome home, Stewart. Notice
how the lawn rebelled since dawn.
Swollen on dew, new weeds wait

for weeding—go change your clothes.
I am tedium and a grout brush. But home,
our home, must not mean your meantime.

The runner rug bunches in the hall
and no one finds time to straighten it
until the second no one falls.

The mess is clear. Every day, disarray
grows more patterned, and I grow too
to hate the half-assed way you hack

at trumpet vines. Theirs is an earnest onslaught
and your hatchet work is a hatchet job.
Good god. The Ace store stocks poisons

ten high, aisles and aisles of the stuff
with precision sprayers, pistol triggers—
and each an admonishment: *apply, apply!*

THE COUNTY FAIR BUILDING FOR ANIMAL HUSBANDRY

The wire hutches sat empty.
No sateen ribbons or nuzzling rabbits,
no nametags rocking in grit-filled wind
that soothed through the open bay doors.
It was worse than we thought it'd be,

to see no winners, no placers,
no child breeder to proudly tell us
in the half-dusk of concrete pillars
that she alone rose at dawn
to bottle feed each in the blind litter.

We didn't know we wanted rabbits
until we saw there were none to see.
Then, it was almost too late to joke
away the gnawing sense that the fair
had cheated us. We laughed it

off by admiring the bright chest
of a peacock pacing its hay-strewn pen.
We stuffed ourselves on corndogs,
paid to pop a carny's taut balloons,
and labored not to pinpoint all that was amiss.

GUN

The trigger travels half an inch
until the pin slams the primer.
What leaves won't come back,

can't be seen until the aftermath.
Just a crack and a dropped target,
whatever the target.

Pray you'll be glad for that.

The killing ball, the actual bullet,
nests in a jacket, brass is best,
a raptor snug for winter.

An ejected sleeve, sloughed off
the death slug, sounds like a coin
flipped to concrete,

slight as a nickel's *ting.*
Then a high ring or whine.
Whatever's next is whatever's next—

night birds wheeling from trees,
your dog, deaf for years, blinking,
sad in his quiet and confusion—

what's next is fact. Then comes rhetoric.

COOK TAKES STOCK AFTER THE ICE ROAD FAILS

Onion. Rutabaga. Chive.
Beeve sides. Pork hide,
the whisky, boss's red wine
all lost on a stretch of candle ice.
Our good mules, two to a cart.
The yoke strained but yoked
they stayed, a snarl of leather,
flesh, and harness as water rushed
aboard the brittle ice. How the cart
dimmed before the mules did,
both girls heaving against the drag.
Not a thing we could do.
Not ice or men strong enough
to brace against such weight.
From the ice shelf, we yelled
in the first shatter of hooves on ice,
urging our Mollies landward.
The floe tilted the mules like wild messengers
from the steaming churn of water,
icy spray glistening off their shorn manes.
Afterwards, the last slow bubbles lingered.
No sound but ice docking ice.
I swore to the men we beheld baptism.
And what was left us? This: to kneel
at the shore and pray that the provenance
of mercy lies not in the hearts of men alone.

DIVING BELL

She is newly mad
and cut from our rural district.
Uninvited—their word—for lack of staff.
She sailed a fist through the fish tank.

Her parents fade to spent ash
pulling doubles at the pulping plant
where they feed chips and splinters
into chemical vats of hissing slurry.

Home, they erect a swing set of soft pine,
the slide a bowed composite plank.
The lash-up's anchored by her weight
and lilts, a grounded ship's stripped frame.

Inadequate clapper in the cracked bell
of herself, swinging, the girl peals her days,
hitting nothing but the air thickened
by spring, gnats, the lately hatched

and happy bundles of mosquitos.
When she slows, when her feet kick
the dirt from up the worn strip
beneath her perch, she's hazed

in bug life and leans her head
to the swing's warm chain.
It will take years, but this year
it starts: her helixed descent

to the plastic castle, the tiny chest
stuffed with gold, to the skeleton
cased in a diving bell dress
who will shift and grin when she settles.

SOMNILOQUENCE ON THE HIGH PLAINS

When dreams rise from your familial past
of tongue-speakers seared in Holiness
I listen for some sense in the gamboling
vowels and consonants as they spill
from the headwaters of your lips.
The Pentecostal Spirit enflames you.
Come daybreak, you are drawn and wan,
changed, the way Oklahoma's red dust
must have stained the hand-spun hems
of dresses worn by the stalk-thin women
you weigh yourself against, reckoning
nightly in your attic glossolalia a faith
that compels you to seek more rousing fires,
first through grace then by sore travails.
Wet your brow. The lenient city admits you now
from off night's furnace of creosote and shale.

TEXAS, STARVED AND FED

In advance of flame the men churn
deep gouges in the brittle pastures.
They earth up their fire lines,
the bulwarks snaking boulevards
of mounded sand and dirt to save
what herds and fodder they can.
Thick in smoke, the caprock rises
to the east. Red tongues crest,
and the county men watch
the first brace of rabbits skitter
past, touched in ash. One succumbs
at their feet. Stung by a windborne
ember, it gutters in its breath.
Someone coughs. Someone sparks
the propane torch. The backburns
are set—minor fires sent to shore
the line, to starve out the blaze.

WHAT YOU'LL MISS, YOU'LL MISS

Across summer's tundra
of bind weed and macadam,
cicada click like Geiger counters
or rattlesnakes. But keep past
the last fence and its rent house,
past Jessup's Gas & Grocery, gutted
as vine and strangler's grass yoke
it back to earth, termites, and dust.
It's easy to miss the honeylocust
circling the last crumbling bricks.
That field was quit before you were born.
It's easier still to miss
what once stood there.
But if it's let go, your focus can sense
the twin-rut trace leading first
to a playhouse raised from scrapwood
and tin, then the farmhouse,
sturdy as the day they hung the horseshoe.
Forget those fantasies now.
You won't draw water, but the well
is real. Test me: stand, hands
splayed above the rotten cap
like they're warming at a fire,
and feel the damp sigh rise
from its moss-lined gut,
faint as a nightmare you had
decades ago that left you
and leaves you still with an ache.
It rises in line at the post office:
this fear you will never have your say
in what will stand and what must fail
in the far reaches, without fanfare,
with no witness to wring his hands
and wince. No one to sing *tsk tsk.*

STARING DOWN

Vicious dawn, I'm better off behind your trued sights
    than before, smelling of sawdust and graphite.

WHAT'S NEW FOR THE INCUNABULIST

Love, for one. Quietly, without fanfare
and little conversation between them
the restoration specialist
feels something spread from the white
middle of his chest.
The way paper foxes in a vault,
the living mold across wire and chain
lines in the archives of a city
dogged by damp air off a great lake.
Nothing's newer than love. Nothing
older, either, and thus befuddled
the specialist sticks to his study
of typesets, how ligatures link
two letters and, once pressed, refuse
to let them disconnect. If the word
if is a single glyph, all the more to use
those binding finials for *then*
or *perhaps,* or even *pears,* the fruit
he compares to her imagined shoulders
in the minutes he's slipping toward sleep.
She's showing him how to set a stick,
words that lay in a chain,
leading on like a bridge over a body
of water so vast the days are lost
in its crossing. To arrive is to be
so glad that he'll turn to admire
the distance before he crosses back.

LOSING GROUND

Because the drought holds nothing
but theft in its mind it can keep
the dirt it harries east and skyward,
unearthing some child's lost cache:
two steelies, and an ought-three domino
with flecks of black paint in its pips
anchored to the few shallow hollows.
I rinse my finds with the hose.

The tawny stain on the domino remains.
The steelies, though, shine up fine,
two more hard eyes. In my palm,
they glint above our dryland spread.
I hold them up. We survey what we're left.

THE BESIEGED ARE OFTEN SAVED BY WATER

After he jacks the pump
the spigot groans, cold water fills
his cupped hands, overruns them,
splashing off finely ground gravel
in a spray of cool mist.
It's a good well he's augured.
It reaches a deep line and doesn't freeze
or lend the bitter tang of metal
to the pool leaking from his pooled
hands. At the tree line, elms picket
his clearing, their roots reach
for the cistern's crumbling walls
to breach then drain its contents.
When he draws the cupped water
upward, the cuffs of his shirt darken,
and he drinks too the dirt loosed
from the palms' grooves. From the side,
it looks like prayer. From behind,
like his chest hitches, like he's sobbing.

NIGHT STUDIES: *LAUDO, LAUDARE, LAUDAVI, LAUDATUM*

Left in the blue dark of our living room,
my wife's Latin grammar bulges with loose-leaf
marked in her looping hand, a manuscript
of anxieties and flecks of graphite ash.
Her night studies I like better: eyes shut,
she chants the verb's progressions,

trills them through her teeth. The lilt
of their forms rising like a late prayer
in a late church poised on ruin,
or the forms are birdsong of want,
each a decade above our shared bed
late and late and late until it's Monday

and our city sloughs back from sand.
I feign sleep—*I praise, to praise
I have praised, having been praised*—
and mouth the sounds beside her.

THE VINE KNIFE

Another strain in the fabric
of days already chafed
to corded threads like work
pants I wore so long
my vine knife's heft
rubbed through a belt loop.
That, for it, was that,

lost to rust in Elder's patch
or dropped to a barroom floor
once the last strings eased
and the loop became a strap.

The lack of its honest weight
at my waist a grief that spiked
as I kicked a late melon's skull.
Harvest closed. Then came snow.

A SAPLING ON THE PLAINS

Bad place for a nest, bird.
You're bound to grow bent

like the dogwood, fly awry
when you find the wind

dies down. When it gusts
watch you aren't plucked

from flight and impaled
on a picket. Your birdy guts

bleeding down the grimed paint.
Observe that smarter bird,

its nest in the nook of a trellis.
The lattice, roughly hewn,

perhaps, offers a safer shelf,
the lee a burst of trumpet vines

to buffer these feculent winds.
Stay, and your song will lose its mind.

WE ARE FEWER THAN BEFORE

in memoriam, LR

He checks the obits from his old town
for the ghost of himself he finds there,
to compare notes for what he should
recall and what he knows was true.
That girl he left seizing in a bathtub
(a fine foam spittle, tiny soap bubbles
rising from cherry-glossed lips,
her benediction, a shallow gurgle
telling him it's fine to leave) survived
that time but not this later one.
And he wonders if the new friend
plucked the spike before he called,
if he pulled her sleeve to hide the tracks,
faked discovery as though he just arrived.
Or if surviving was punishment enough.
And he pulled shut each door as he left
and left and could not stop leaving.
If he's sadder now. Tired, and more free.

IF THERE'S NOTHING YOU NEED

Suppose I'll go then to the hardware store
where they still hang steel buckets for bulk nails
to weigh and bag in a small paper sack.
Wander past chain links wound tight on wooden
spools. And rope displays. If I test its rough threads,
the hewn braid snaps taut in my hands. Pulling
shroud-laid twine through a fist I clench

a flame that burns from nothing. My raw palm.
I need the industry of things, flat heads
heavy in a breast pocket, their points cut
the bag, my shirt when I find you alone
watching the road, and force a long embrace.

THE LEAST OF WONDERS

This bok schal afterward ben ended
Of love, which doth many a wonder
–Gower

Years later, the neighbor seems like kin
to St. Francis of Assisi, a lost relation,
and the most humane among us.
In our subdivision of subprime rates,
the salt-crusted cars sped past her
as she scattered kibble, and the tins
of wet food she left the cats
were soon empty, wind snagged
to tumble down the frozen lawns.

Now another fall is turning.
The colony she tended that worst winter
is long joined to legions of their dead.
But I can see her stab at the frozen water
with her dead husband's screwdriver, clucking
gibberish to her wards when they'd rush
from their blanket-draped boxes,
figure-eighting her legs, waiting
for the thaw of mercy. Even now
I am easily shamed and wrench

my neck back to watch her efforts.
My mother was driving me somewhere—
Mass, school, or a practice I can't recall.
The demands of that day are lost,
and still I square myself by that widow,
small at the work, alone and in the cold.

Grateful acknowledgement is made to the editors of the following publications where these poems first appeared, sometimes in different versions:

AGNI: "*Confessio Inimicus*" and "A Paper Hive Earns No Quarter"
Blackbird: "Cook Takes Stock after the Ice Road Fails"
Cave Wall: "We'd Learn Later Her Husband Left" and "Texas, Starved and Fed"
Cortland Review: "Considerations on Making Odds for the Iditarod"
Cutbank: "Bee: Late Season"
Harpur Palate: "Stray" (as "Toward the Eastern Seaboard")
Hawai'i Pacific Review: "North Is Looking Up"
Hayden's Ferry Review: "Bird. Pilgrim. Water."
Iron Horse Literary Review: "Elegy with Cigarettes and Folding Chairs"
Jelly Bucket: "Gun"
Linebreak: "If There's Nothing You Need"
The Louisville Review: "The Besieged Are often Saved by Water"
MARGIE: "Begging Home a Stray"
Meridian: "What's New for the Incunabulist"
The National Poetry Review: "On Touching My Dog's Cold and Perfect Teeth"
Natural Bridge: "The Future Timber Baron Writes His New Wife"
Poet Lore: "Night Studies: *Laudo, Laudare, Laudavi, Laudatum*"
Portland Review: "How My Grandfather Thought about Intelligent Design"
Post Road: "The County Fair Building for Animal Husbandry"
and "We Are Fewer than Before"
Permafrost: "Diving Bell"
Roanoke Review: "Somniloquence on the High Plains"
Shenandoah: "The One Where the Girl Died in Woods Close to Home"
The Southeast Review: "The Reddish Cur"
Superstition Review: "Gunflint Range" (as "The First Night of Spring
in the Gunflint Range")
Tar River Poetry: "A Sapling on the Plains"
Willow Springs: "To the Bed Bug"
Valparaiso Poetry Review: "The Vine Knife"

"The Reddish Cur" appeared in *Best New Poets 2010* (University of Virginia, Meridian Press), edited by Claudia Emerson

"Begging Home a Stray" and "After Watching a K-9 Assault Demonstration at Lackland AFB, 1967" appeared in the anthology *Dogs Singing* (Salmon Poetry), edited by Jessie Lendennie

"The Slow Promenade of Armadillos" appeared in the anthology *Improbable Worlds* (Mutabilis Press), edited by Martha Serpas

"Somniloquence on the High Plains," and "We'd Learn Later Her Husband Left" appeared in the anthology *Gathered* (Sun Dress Publications), edited by Nick McRae

My abiding gratitude to the teachers and friends for their careful eyes and the time they generously gave to help these poems along the way.

Thank you to Curtis Bauer, George David Clark, Anthony Frame, Austin Hummell, Jonathan Bohr Heinen, Jackie Kolosov, Rhonda Lott, Beverly Matherne, Michelle Menting, Brent Newsom, Rick Pierce, John Poch, Jake Ricafrente, Eric Smith, Casey Thayer, and Bill Wenthe.

Thank you to Danny Rosen and Kyle Harvey at Lithic Press for believing in the book and making it happen.

My love, too, to my parents and my sisters for their support and good cheer, and to Emma, who needed nothing and brought so much. She is missed.

Lastly, my gratitude, my love, and my thanks to Landon Houle, for whom the labor means.

Adam Houle's poems have appeared in journals such as *AGNI, Shenandoah, Guernica, Barrow Street, Post Road, Cave Wall, Poet Lore, Blackbird, Hayden's Ferry Review,* and his fiction can be found in *Cimarron Review.* Claudia Emerson selected his work for *Best New Poets 2010.* Nominated for both a Pushcart and for Best of the Net, he was also a semi-finalist for the *Boston Review* / "Discovery" Prize and a finalist for the *Art & Letters* Rumi Prize in Poetry. He earned a PhD from Texas Tech and currently lives in Darlington, South Carolina with writer and editor Landon Houle.